IT'S COOL TO LEARN ABOUT COUNTRIES

Social Studies Explorer

PHILIPPINES

⊷ by Vicky Franchino

CHERRY LAKE PUBLISHING • ANN ARBOR, MICHIGAN

Published in the United States of America
by Cherry Lake Publishing
Ann Arbor, Michigan
www.cherrylakepublishing.com

Content Adviser: Michael Cullinane, PhD, Associate Professor,
University of Wisconsin-Madison

Book design: The Design Lab

Photo credits: Cover and pages 3, 10 top, 13 top, 16 top, 21 top, 22 top, 27 right, 37 top, 39 top, 41 top, and 48, ©iStockphoto.com/PictureLake; cover and pages 8 bottom, 10 bottom, 13 bottom, 15, 27 left, 39 bottom, and 41 bottom, ©iStockphoto.com/bluestocking; cover and page 12, ©JJ Morales/Shutterstock, Inc.; pages 4, 11, and 45, ©Antonio V. Oquias/Shutterstock, Inc.; pages 5 and 37 bottom, ©iStockphoto.com/simongurney; page 6, ©iStockphoto.com/BrettCharlton; page 8 top, ©Disiflections/Dreamstime.com; page 9, ©iStockphoto.com/ktrifonov; page 16 bottom, ©Ragsac19/Dreamstime.com; page 17, ©Allan Szeto/Shutterstock, Inc.; page 18, ©The Art Gallery Collection/Alamy; page 19, ©Tonyoquias/Dreamstime.com; pages 20 and 21 bottom, ©AP Photo/Aaron Favila; page 23, ©Steve coulson/Alamy; page 25, ©Marc F. Henning/Alamy; page 26, ©iStockphoto.com/tonyoquias; page 28, ©Joeygil/Dreamstime.com; page 29, ©Shadow216/Dreamstime.com; page 31, ©Jon Arnold Images Ltd/Alamy; page 32, ©Arco Images GmbH/Alamy; page 36, ©Emma Wood/Alamy; page 38, ©Thomas Cockrem/Alamy; page 40, ©Rolenf/Dreamstime.com; page 42, ©Deddeda Deddeda/photolibrary; page 43, ©iStockphoto.com/tazytaz

Library of Congress Cataloging-in-Publication Data
Franchino, Vicky.
  It's cool to learn about countries: Philippines/by Vicky Franchino.
     p. cm.—(Social studies explorer)
  Includes bibliographical references and index.
  ISBN-13: 978-1-60279-834-2 (lib. bdg.)
  ISBN-10: 1-60279-834-6 (lib. bdg.)
  1. Philippines—Juvenile literature. I. Title. II. Title: Philippines. III. Series.
  DS655.F73 2010
  959.9—dc22   2010005509

Cherry Lake Publishing would like to acknowledge the work of The Partnership for 21st Century Skills. Please visit www.21stcenturyskills.org for more information.

Printed in the United States of America
Corporate Graphics Inc.
July 2010
CLFA07

TABLE OF CONTENTS

RICE FOR PROGRESS

CHAPTER ONE

WELCOME TO THE PHILIPPINES!

➥ Boats are a common sight in the waters of the Philippines.

Have you ever wanted to visit a country in which the weather is always warm? Where there are hundreds of kinds of birds, animals, and plants? Where you could pick a banana to eat for breakfast? Then you might like to visit the Philippines!

The Philippines is filled with tropical rainforests, towering mountains, and beautiful beaches. If you traveled to the Philippines, you probably wouldn't need to take a heavy coat. That's because it is hot and humid all year round. But you might need an umbrella if you're traveling during the rainy season. You would certainly want to take your binoculars, too, because there are a lot of amazing things to see. Let's learn more about the Philippines.

The Philippines has many interesting places to explore.

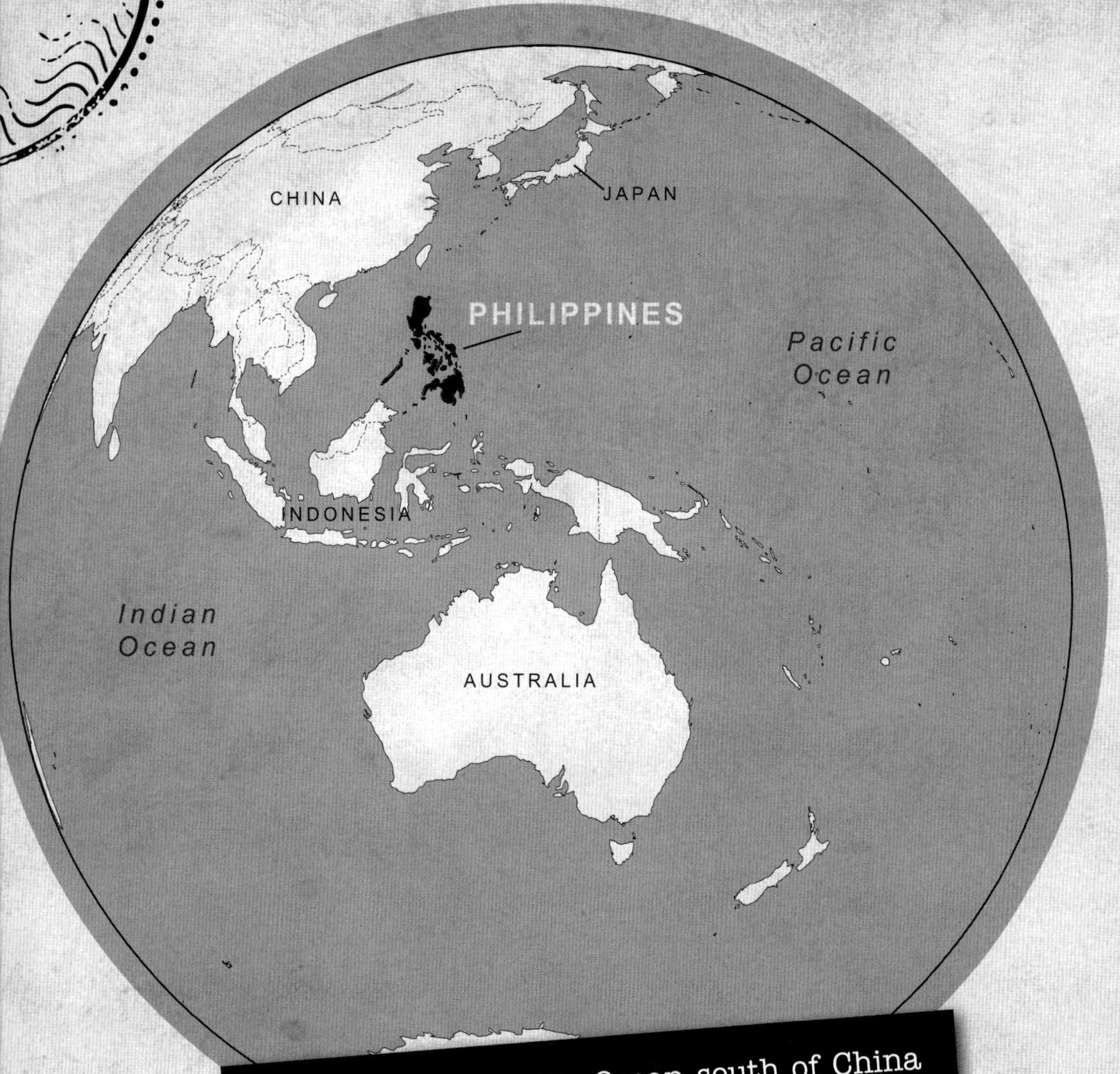

CHINA

JAPAN

PHILIPPINES

Pacific
Ocean

INDONESIA

Indian
Ocean

AUSTRALIA

❧ Look in the Pacific Ocean south of China
to find the islands of the Philippines.

Where will you find the Philippines on a globe or a
map? The nation is within Southeast Asia. It's made up
of a large group of islands, called an **archipelago**. Just
how many islands are there? More than 7,000!

That's a lot of islands. But most of them are very small. Put the islands together and the country is approximately the size of Arizona, but a lot more crowded. More than 90 million people live in the Philippines. Manila, or Metro Manila, is the capital.

◦◦ Manila is a large and busy city.

Although there are more than 7,000 islands that make up the Philippines, most maps show a lot fewer. Trace the islands you see here. Label Manila. Use an atlas or find a map online that will help you label the three main groups of islands: Luzon, the Visayas, and Mindanao. Label Mount Mayon and Mount Pinatubo, too. These are two famous volcanoes.

The Philippines is approximately 116,000 square miles (300,000 square kilometers) in area. Because it is made up of islands, the Philippines has one of the longest coastlines of any country. If you like to go to the beach, you can certainly find one in the Philippines. Most of the country is mountainous. The highest point is Mount Apo, which is 9,692 feet (2,954 meters) high.

The Chocolate Hills sound delicious, don't they? These smooth hills turn brown during the dry season and look like giant chocolate cones!

Chocolate Hills

Much of the Philippines usually experiences warm weather. Temperatures can vary depending on the season and region. The average temperature in the lowlands, for example, is approximately 80 degrees Fahrenheit (26.7 degrees Celsius). The mountains and upland areas, however, experience cooler temperatures.

The Philippines is located in part of an area known as the Ring of Fire. It is an appropriate name for the zone because many volcanic eruptions and earthquakes occur there.

The Philippines has dry seasons and wet seasons. During the wet season, heavy winds called monsoons bring rainstorms. There are also violent storms called typhoons, which are similar to hurricanes.

Because temperatures are so warm, many different types of birds, animals, and plants can live in the Philippines. Pollution, **erosion**, and **deforestation**, however, are taking a toll on the habitat of many of the Philippines' living treasures. Fortunately, certain groups work hard to protect the country's wildlife.

❧ Forests are often cleared so the land can be used for farming.

CHAPTER TWO

BUSINESS AND GOVERNMENT IN THE PHILIPPINES

➥ Rice is sometimes grown on leveled terraces that are carved into hills and mountains.

How do Filipinos support themselves? For much of the country's history, most people were farmers or fishermen. The rich volcanic soil of the country is good for growing many crops. Some include rice, sugarcane, coconuts, and bananas. Pineapples, **cassavas**, and corn are some other crops. Rice and fish are staple foods for much of the population.

You probably eat fruit that comes from the Philippines. Find a can of pineapple or mandarin oranges in your cupboards. Inspect the label. There's a good chance you'll discover that your fruit has traveled a long way!

Filipino factories produce many goods, including clothing, medicines, and computer parts. The Philippines sends many of its **exports** to China, the United States, and Japan. Also, many Filipinos work overseas.

IMPORT EXPORT

Do you want to know more about the Philippines' economy? Then take a look at its trading partners. Trading partners are the countries that **import** goods from a country or export goods to that country. Here is a graph showing the countries that are the Philippines' top import and export trading partners.

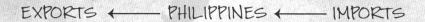

EXPORTS ⟵ PHILIPPINES ⟵ IMPORTS

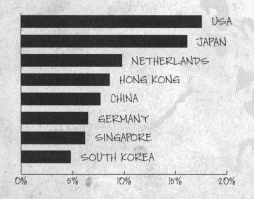

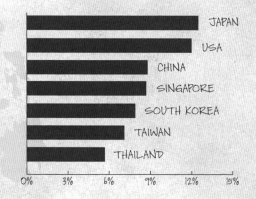

Approximately half of Filipino workers have a job in a service industry. This means that they don't make or grow a product. Instead, they provide a service. People who work for the government or in a store are just a few examples of service employees.

ACTIVITY

A pie chart is one way to compare data. In the Philippines, 50% of workers provide services. Roughly 35% have jobs related to agriculture. Approximately 15% have jobs related to industry. Using this labor force information, create a pie chart. Ask an adult for help if you need it.

STOP
Don't write in this book!

The Philippines is a country of great contrasts. If you went to a big city such as Manila, you would see skyscrapers. But you might also spot shacks made of tin that don't have running water or electricity. Approximately one out of every three people lives in poverty.

The Philippine unit of money is called the piso or Philippine peso. In 2010, one U.S. dollar equaled approximately 45.8 Philippine pesos.

•➤ Spanish colonists built forts like this one all across the Philippines.

The Philippines has been a colony of two countries: Spain and the United States. The country was a Spanish colony from the 1500s until 1898. The Philippines declared they were no longer a Spanish colony on June 12, 1898. That year Spain fought a war with the United States.

The Philippines got its name when it was a Spanish colony. It was named after King Philip II of Spain.

King Philip II

The Philippines fought on the side of the United States in the hope that it would help the nation stay independent. Spain lost the war. Spain surrendered the Philippines to the United States for $20 million. Filipinos were angry at not being granted independence. Soon, the United States and the Philippines would battle each other in the Filipino-American War. The Philippines became a U.S. colony.

The United States gave the Philippines total independence on July 4, 1946. For many years, the Philippines celebrated independence on the same day as the United

States—July 4. Today, it is celebrated on the day the country became independent from Spain: June 12.

Since independence, the Philippines has had two forms of government. A **democratic** system based on elections has been used between 1946 and 1972, and between 1986 and the present. The nation was under an **authoritarian** system dominated by President Ferdinand Marcos and the military between 1972 and 1986.

•◇ Independence Day celebrations are filled with the national colors of red, blue, and yellow.

The democratic system of government features three branches. The executive branch includes the president and the vice president. In the United States, these two people are from the same political party. They are elected as a team. In the Philippines, voters choose a president and a vice president and they might come from different political parties. The president and vice president are elected for one term that lasts 6 years.

→ President Gloria Macapagal Arroyo delivers a speech to Congress.

The Philippine government has had two female presidents. The first was Corazon Aquino. Corazon was the wife of Beniquo Aquino, Jr. He opposed the dictatorship of Ferdinand Marcos. After Beniquo was killed by government soldiers, Corazon ran against Marcos in the 1986 election. Before the election, many Filipinos took part in a nonviolent protest against Marcos. Corazon became president. The second female president was Gloria Macapagal Arroyo. She took over the presidency in 2001 after the previous president was pressured to step down due to corruption charges. She was elected to serve a full term in 2004.

Gloria Macapagal Arroyo

The legislative branch has a Senate and a House of Representatives that make the country's laws. The judicial branch has 15 justices who interpret the laws of the country.

The Philippine flag has a band of blue that stands for peace and justice. The red band represents patriotism and courage. The white triangle represents equality. A sun and stars are within the triangle. The eight rays of the sun stand for the **provinces** that fought for independence from Spain. The three stars represent the nation's major island groups of Luzon, the Visayas, and Mindanao. During times of peace, the flag is flown with the blue stripe on top. During war, the red stripe is on top.

CHAPTER THREE

MEET THE PEOPLE

❖ Many families have lived in the Philippines for generations.

Through the years, many different people have settled in the Philippines. Some groups arrived from the continent of Asia 20,000 to 30,000 years ago. Scientists believe there may once have been land bridges connecting the Philippines to Asia. These land bridges were exposed when ocean levels dropped. This would have allowed people to walk to the Philippines!

Malay groups came to the Philippines by boat from the Malay and Indonesian islands. Most of today's Filipinos are at least part Malay.

Experts generally estimate that 80 languages exist in the Philippines. Tagalog is the language spoken in Manila and its surrounding areas. It is considered the basis of the country's national language. It is taught as "Filipino" in all public and private schools today. English is another major language. Most Filipinos speak three languages: their own local language, Filipino (Tagalog), and English.

FILIPINO

Some Filipino words are very similar to Spanish words. Can you can match the Filipino and Spanish words for the days of the week? See below for the answers.

Filipino	Spanish
1) Lúnes (Monday)	a) miércoles
2) Martés (Tuesday)	b) viernes
3) Miyérkules (Wednesday)	c) lunes
4) Huwébes (Thursday)	d) sábado
5) Biyérnes (Friday)	e) martes
6) Sábado (Saturday)	f) domingo
7) Linggó (Sunday)	g) jueves

Answers: 1-c; 2-e; 3-a; 4-g; 5-b; 6-d; 7-f

Since the 15th century, peoples—mostly traders—from other parts of the world have settled in the Philippines. They were mainly Chinese, Arab, Indian, and European. Many intermarried with native peoples, creating large numbers of people of mixed ethnicity. They would come to be called *mestizos*.

❧ Classes are usually taught in Filipino or English.

◆ Most Filipinos worship in Catholic churches.

Islam arrived in the Philippines before Christianity. The religion was spread largely by Islamic traders of Arab and Indian descent. By the 15th century, three major ethnic groups of the southern islands had adopted Islam. Today, approximately 5 percent of Filipinos are Muslim.

Beginning in 1565, Spanish **missionaries** brought the Catholic religion to the Philippines. Over the next 200

years, many converted to Christianity. Today, more than 90 percent of Filipinos are Christian. Most are Catholic.

Filipinos value education. More than 92 percent of the population knows how to read. Children go to elementary school from the ages of 6 through 12. They attend high school between the ages of 13 and 16. Even though children are required to attend elementary school, not all of them do. There might not be a school nearby. Or their parents might need their help at home or with a family business.

As in many parts of the world, class and political differences have sometimes led to conflicts in the Philippines. Even so, Filipinos try hard to get along with others. Pakikisama can be translated as "getting along with one another." Bayanihan implies working together to get a job done. These traditional values are taught in schools.

CHAPTER FOUR

CELEBRATIONS

◆ Town festivals often include traditional dances, clothing, and music.

Filipinos like to get together with family and friends for celebrations. Many celebrations are tied to religious events.

Every village has a celebration in honor of its patron saint. The people believe that the saint protects their village in a special way. During the celebration there

are usually parades, food, and music. There are many other celebrations that go along with Christian holidays.

Christmas honors the birth of Jesus Christ. Celebrations start on December 16. Christmas falls on December 25, and the Feast of the Three Kings is on January 6.

In the spring, Christians remember the last days of Jesus Christ's life during a 40-day period known as Lent. Many towns have a *sinakulo*. This is a play about the life and death of Jesus.

❧ The Feast of the Black Nazarene is one of the biggest religious celebrations in the Philippines.

Muslims also have important religious holidays. One is the *hari-raya poasa*. It comes at the end of Ramadan, which is the holiest time of the Muslim year. Throughout Ramadan, people don't eat between sunrise and sunset. During the hari-raya poasa celebration, Muslims pray, visit the graves of loved ones, and enjoy time with family.

HOLIDAYS

These are some holidays that are celebrated in the Philippines:

New Year's Day	January 1
Holy Thursday	March or April
Good Friday	March or April
Easter Sunday	March or April
Labor Day	May 1
Independence Day	June 12
Filipino-American Friendship Day	July 4
hari-raya poasa	End of Ramadan
Bonifacio Day	Monday nearest November 30
Christmas	December 25
Rizal Day	Monday nearest December 30

Filipinos often wear casual clothes such as jeans and T-shirts. When it's time for a celebration, however, traditional clothes are very popular. Men wear a special shirt called a *barong tagalog*. This shirt is not tucked in. It's covered with beautiful **embroidery**.

Women sometimes wear a long skirt known as a *saya*. Or they might wear a dress called a *terno*. It is a combination of a long-sleeved blouse and a saya.

➥ Traditional clothing is often worn on special occasions.

For fun, Filipino children like to play games. They might fly a *boka-boka*, which is a small kite. *Luksong-tinik* is another popular pastime. This is a game in which players jump over a stick or the outstretched arms of other players.

↝ Sungka is a traditional game played on a wooden board.

CRAFT ACTIVITY

Try making your own boka-boka kite.

MATERIALS

- 1 sheet of paper, 8.5 inches x 11 inches (21.6 centimeters by 27.9 cm)
- Crayons or markers
- Thread
- Tape
- Pencil
- Ruler
- Scissors

INSTRUCTIONS

1. Lay the piece of paper on a flat work surface, with one of the shorter sides closest to you. Using a pencil, label the shorter side farthest from you, "A." Label the shorter side closest to you, "B." Label the long side to the left, "C" and the long side to the right, "D."

2. Decorate the paper however you like using crayons or markers.

3. Place your paper in front of you, with the decorated side facing up and side B closest to you.

Instructions on the following page →

4. Take a ruler and measure 2.5 inches (6.4 cm) from the edge of Side B. Draw a line parallel to side B across your paper at that point. Draw another parallel line 2.5 inches (6.4 cm) from side A.

5. Fold your paper along each of these lines, so that the "A" and "B" labels are folded under and facing the tabletop.

6. Turn your paper over so that the decorated side is face-down. Side C should be closest to you.

7. Start with the left-hand flap. Measure 2.5 inches (6.4 cm) up from the edge of side C. Mark this spot with a pencil. Repeat this step with the right-hand flap.

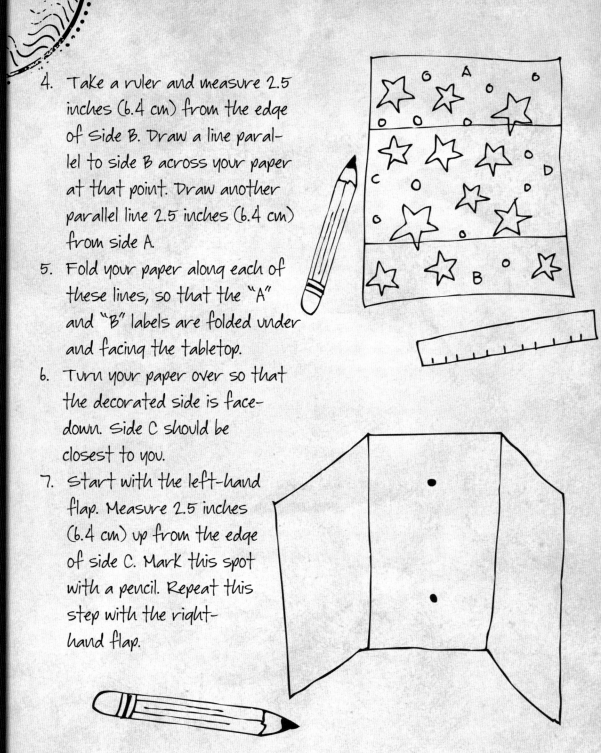

8. Using scissors, cut a piece of thread that is 44 inches (111.8 cm) long.

9. Tape one end of the thread to the left-hand pencil mark. Tape the other end to the right-hand pencil mark. You should now have a loop of string attached to the kite.

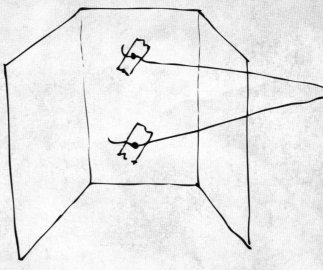

10. Turn your kite over.

11. Cut another piece of thread that is 5 feet (1.5 meters) long.

12. Thread this piece of string through the loop that's attached to the kite. This will be what you hold on to as you fly the kite. Tie the ends of the thread into a knot.

You are now ready to fly your kite!

➡ Sipa is sometimes played with a net.

Pabitin is very popular with children. Prizes are hung from a frame that is raised or lowered while the children try to reach for the prizes.

Sipa is a traditional sport. You may have played a similar game called Hacky Sack. The goal is to see who can kick the ball the most times before letting it hit the ground. The ball can only touch players' legs from the knee down. Children can play by themselves or with friends. The game can also be played by teams with more formal rules.

Just like people around the world, Filipinos enjoy many different sports and pastimes. Basketball and boxing are two popular sports in the Philippines.

You've probably seen a yellow cab. But have you ever seen a rainbow one? In the Philippines, you can find very colorful cabs called jeepneys. Jeepneys can usually hold more than 10 people. Their owners paint them very bright colors and decorate them.

CHAPTER FIVE

WHAT'S FOR DINNER?

SPECIAL GOTO AND NATIVE SNACKS

PAY AS YOU ORDER PLEASE

Special GOTO 29.00 only

Gloria's PALABOK 32.00 only

SAGO/GULAMAN 10.00

➥ Have you ever tried Filipino food?

If you could walk among the food vendors in the Philippines, you'd see that Filipino food blends many different cultures. Some types of food are similar to Chinese dishes. Others might remind you of Spanish or American foods.

Recipes made with noodles are often based on foods that came from China. The Spanish brought ingredients such as olive oil and ham. Filipinos used them to make interesting new dishes.

Filipinos have their own version of fast food. It is called turo-turo. The word turo means "to point." Customers visit food vendors who have a number of dishes arranged on a table. They point to the ones they would like to eat.

→ Like many dishes, adobo usually comes with a serving of rice.

No matter what or when you eat, you'll probably have rice with your meal. Dishes that might traditionally be served with corn or potatoes in other countries are often served with rice in the Philippines.

If you like Asian food, but are not a fan of hot chili peppers, you should try Filipino dishes. Most do not incorporate hot peppers, unlike the foods of many other Southeast Asian countries. Some common foods you'll find in the Philippines include *suman*. These are rice

cakes. They are wrapped in coconut or banana leaves and cooked using steam. *Adobo* is a popular stew made of pork or chicken. It has a flavorful sauce. On a special occasion, you might get to enjoy a delicious dessert called *halo-halo*. It's made of fruit, milk, chunks of ice, and gelatin. Sometimes it includes boiled sweet beans. No celebration is complete without *lechón*. This is a young pig that is roasted for many hours on a spit.

If you go on a picnic in the Philippines, there might not be any paper plates in the picnic basket. There might be banana leaves instead!

banana leaves

Sit down for a meal in the Philippines and you might use a fork and spoon or chopsticks. Sometimes you might get to eat with your hands. This way of eating is called *kamayan*. There is a special way to do it.

Use your fingertips to make a small ball of rice. Pick up a piece of chicken, fish, or whatever else is part of your meal. Put it on top of the rice ball. Make sure the ball isn't too big! Lift the ball to your mouth, keeping your fingers close together. Push the food ball into your mouth with your thumb. It will take some practice to get it just right.

➺ Pancit is a popular noodle dish

Pancit is a dish made with thin rice noodles. This recipe is a great way to use up leftover meat. You could also use extra vegetables instead of chicken or pork if you don't eat meat. This recipe requires chopping ingredients and using a stove. Be sure to ask an adult for help.

Pancit

INGREDIENTS

A 12-ounce (340 grams) package dried rice noodles, broken into pieces

1 teaspoon (4.9 milliliters) vegetable oil

3 green onions, sliced

1 to 2 teaspoons (3.2 to 6.3 grams) chopped garlic

3 cups cabbage, thinly sliced

2 cups diced, cooked chicken breast or pork

4 carrots, thinly sliced

¼ cup (59.1 ml) soy sauce

2 lemons, cut into wedges for garnish

INSTRUCTIONS

1. Place the noodles
   in a large bowl
   and cover them
   with warm water.
   Soak for 25 to 30
   minutes or until the
   noodles are soft.
2. Drain the noodles using
   a colander and set them aside.
3. Have an adult heat the oil in a
   large skillet over medium heat.
4. Add the onion and garlic and cook
   until soft.
5. Use tongs to stir in the meat, cabbage,
   carrots, and soy sauce.
6. Cook until the cabbage is soft.
7. Add the noodles and stir.
8. Cook until everything is thoroughly heated.
9. Place the pancit on a serving dish. Arrange the lemon wedges
   around the edge of the dish

   Enjoy this delicious taste of the Philippines. Better yet, invite
your family and friends to enjoy it with you in true Philippine
style!

The large cluster of islands known as the Philippines has captured the imagination of many people through the years. Has it captured yours yet?

➥ There's always more to learn about the Philippines!

GLOSSARY

archipelago (ar-kuh-PEL-uh-goh) a large group or chain of islands

authoritarian (uh-thor-uh-TAIR-ee-uhn) having to do with the idea that leaders have the final authority or power instead of the people

cassavas (kuh-SAH-vuhz) the roots of a starch-producing plant

deforestation (dee-for-iss-TAY-shuhn) the cutting down of forests

democratic (dem-uh-KRAT-ik) having to do with a political system in which the people elect leaders to represent them in government

embroidery (em-BROI-dur-ee) designs stitched onto cloth

erosion (i-ROH-zhuhn) a gradual wearing away of something by wind, water, or glaciers

exports (EK-sportss) act of selling something to another country or products sold in this way

import (IM-port) bring in from another country

missionaries (MISH-uh-ner-eez) people sent by a religious group to teach their faith in a foreign country

provinces (PROV-uhnss-iz) regions of certain countries

FOR MORE INFORMATION

Books

Drevitch, Gary. *Asia*. New York: Children's Press, 2009.

Skog, Jason. *Teens in the Philippines*. Minneapolis: Compass Point Books, 2009.

Snyder, Gail. *Filipino Americans*. Philadelphia: Mason Crest Publishers, 2009.

Web Sites

Central Intelligence Agency—The World Factbook: Philippines
www.cia.gov/library/publications/the-world-factbook/geos/rp.html
Make use of this great resource for information about the Philippines' government, people, and more.

Save the Children—Philippines—Just for Kids
www.savethechildren.org/countries/asia/philippines-kids.html
Learn some Filipino phrases.

TIME for Kids—Sightseeing Guide—Philippines
www.timeforkids.com/TFK/teachers/aw/wr/article/0,28138,1895686,00.html
Explore an interactive map and learn more about the Philippines.

INDEX

ABOUT THE AUTHOR
Vicky Franchino decided to learn about the Philippines because she has a good friend who was born there. She always thought it was interesting that her friend's last name sounded Hispanic. Now that she knows more about the Philippines, she understands why it does! Vicky lives in Madison, Wisconsin, with her family.